The
Singing Island

The Singing Island
The story of Tiritiri Matangi

Lynnette Moon
Photographs by Geoff Moon

Dedicated to all the keepers of the island

My special thanks to Ray and Barbara Walter for much willing
assistance, to my husband Geoff Moon for all his encouragement,
and my thanks also to Dr David Bellamy.
I am grateful to Ray Richards, Jane Connor and Sarah Bowden
for their enthusiasm. It has been a delight to work with the Godwit team.

A GODWIT BOOK
Published by
Random House New Zealand
18 Poland Road, Glenfield, Auckland, New Zealand

First published 1998

© 1998 Lynnette Moon (text), Geoff Moon (photographs)

ISBN 1 86962 033 X

Design: Sarah Bowden
Front cover photograph: North Island kokako
Back cover photographs: saddleback (left), takahe and chick (right).
Printed in Hong Kong

Contents

Foreword, David Bellamy   6

The Singing Island   8

Appendix 1: Important Food Trees and Shrubs   50

Appendix 2: Birds of Tiritiri Matangi   56

Tiritiri Matangi: An Open Sanctuary   58

How to get there   59

Supporters of Tiritiri Matangi   59

Further Reading   60

Foreword

This is a delightful book, which shows that anything is possible if only people care.

Less than a millennium ago, Tiritiri Matangi, an island off the coast of metro Auckland, was a magical place resplendent with native plants and birds. As with the rest of Aotearoa New Zealand, the only mammals were bats, so it was a safe haven for nesting birds, whose dawn chorus must have been second to none in the world.

Then people arrived on the scene, bringing with them an assortment of alien mammals and plants: dogs, rats, cats, sheep, cows and non-native grasses, to name but a few.

So when I first knew the Singing Island, it was a sad place: overgrazed, its soils compacted, its tiny scraps of native bush losing the one-sided battle against a surfeit of ferals.

On my return some ten years later, the island was beginning to sing again. Along with many school children, I helped to plant a thousand native trees and shrubs, which had been raised from seed collected from the island. The ranger and his wife, Mr and Mrs Walter, inspired us all by telling of a great partnership between the Department of Conservation, The World Wildlife Fund, the Forest and Bird Society, other local groups and, most importantly, many local people, all of whom were heaven bent on bringing that dawn chorus back to sing the praises of Tiritiri Matangi once again.

The magical island, whose name in Maori means 'wind tossing about', now sings the song of the Green Renaissance, and points the way to put the whole world back into working order. All it needs is people who care.

David Bellamy OBE, BSc, PhD, DSc, FLS
Bedburn 1998

Among all the beautiful islands in the world, there is a special island called Tiritiri Matangi. Little rocky bays wrinkle the steep coastline of this long, low island, which lies in the Hauraki Gulf, near Auckland, New Zealand's largest city.

Thousands of years ago the island was a wild place, covered in luxuriant forest and alive with birds, insects and lizards. There were no people on Tiritiri, and the only mammals were bats, so the island was a safe place for birds to feed and nest. Tiritiri belonged to them.

Left: Tiritiri Matangi, showing the indented coastline fringed with pohutukawa trees.

(Brian Moorhead/Focus New Zealand Photo Library)

Forest interior showing kohekohe, which is the dominant tree of the old forest.

Maori were the first to settle on Tiritiri, and they brought with them kiore (rats) and dogs. Clearing away much of the forest, they built houses and grew crops. They caught fish, hunted forest birds, searched out petrel and shearwater chicks, and used some of the island's plants for food. The dogs caught petrels and penguins when they came ashore at night to roost

Above: Grey-faced petrels nest in burrows on coastal headlands.

THE SETTLERS

The first Maori settlers on Tiritiri were from the Kawerau tribe. Archaeological remains of their houses, cooking sheds and kumara-storage pits have been found high on the ridges. On lower land and beach flats the middens or refuse heaps have revealed a wide range of shells and the bones of fish, birds, dogs and kiore. Recent discoveries in the lower layers of the middens have also revealed evidence of moa bones.

Members of the Ngati Paoa tribe later moved into the area, which resulted in friction between the tribes. But with help from another chief, the Kawerau defeated the Ngati Paoa around 1700 and they remained on the island until 1821, when they themselves were forced to flee to the safety of the Waikato on the mainland as Hongi Hika and his warriors approached from the north.

In 1837 the Kawerau began to return to Tiritiri, but by then European settlers had arrived. Both groups felt they had a claim to the island so the matter was brought before the Maori Land Court in 1867 and title was granted to the government.

In 1894 Joseph Schollum obtained a lease from the government to use the land for farming, and after two years this was transferred to Francis Dennis. In 1901 Everard John Hobbs took over the lease and this family connection with Tiritiri lasted for 70 years. The island continued to be farmed, with the scow *Vesper* ferrying cattle and sheep from the island to the Whangaparaoa Peninsula.

In 1947, Everard Hobbs' son John took over the lease until it expired in 1971. The government then decided to hand over responsibility for the island to the Hauraki Gulf Maritime Park Board. Te Kawerau are the tangata whenua of Tiritiri Matangi.

in bracken and burrows, and the kiore took eggs from forest birds' nests, as well as nibbling at seedlings and young shoots.

The birds had known nothing about the trapping, killing ways of people and animals. Now, with the arrival of these new predators, the island was no longer a safe place for them.

These first Maori settlers gave the island its name, Tiritiri Matangi, which means 'a place tossed or moved by the wind'.

Many years later they moved back to the mainland of New Zealand, to escape warriors approaching from the north. Soon after, European settlers arrived on Tiritiri and wanted to clear away even more of the forest in order to farm the island.

So, except for the red-blossomed pohutukawa trees along the shoreline and a little forest that was left on the steep valley slopes, the trees were burnt away. On this cleared land the farmers sowed pasture grasses of cocksfoot and clover to feed their cattle, sheep, goats and pigs. Rabbits also thrived on the open grassland.

Although much of the forest was being cleared away, Tiritiri continued to be used as a roosting place for sea birds as it had been for thousands of years. It did not matter to them whether there was forest or grass on the island. The bushy banks above the shoreline were left alone because they were of no use to the farmers. So by day, sea birds flew freely over the sea, shrilling across and about the island.

Cleared land was planted with pasture grasses of cocksfoot and clover. (Auckland Museum)

Above: Pohutukawa trees are predominant around the island's coast.

Left: White-fronted terns coming in to rest. These birds nest on a reef near the wharf.

THE BLUE PENGUIN

The blue penguin, which is the smallest species of penguin in the world, is common around the New Zealand coast. It swims and dives rapidly through the water, feeding on small fish and crustaceans.

At night, it comes ashore to roost in rocky burrows and will also nest in these or in rock crevices, caves or beneath old tree roots. A few artificial nest sites have been built from rocks and concrete near a track on the foreshore, and these are fitted with viewing panels so visitors can see the birds.

Blue penguins usually lay two eggs, and these are incubated by both parents for 33–40 days. The chicks then fledge when seven or eight weeks old.

Because penguins spend so much of their time in the water, their small wings have been adapted for use as flippers, and their body is covered with a double layer of feathers, the tips overlapping to form a waterproof, protective cover.

And at night, petrels and shearwaters sheltered in their nesting burrows among the brushy shrubs on the steep sea banks.

Blue penguins, which fished in the sea during the day, still flip-flopped ashore at night to sleep snugly in their dry burrows among the rocks. And the gulls, terns and shags that fed at sea during the day often roosted at night on the bare, rocky foreshore.

The old pohutukawa trees which have always grown along the shoreline continued to bloom with their bright red, brush flowers in early summer. Pohutukawa flowers, like flax, kowhai and puriri flowers, are filled with honey-sweet nectar, and tui sometimes flew over from the mainland to feed on them. Tall, wild grasses left around the edges of the pasture provided seeds for other birds like finches, quail and pheasants.

But the forest birds were in trouble. The large trees they depended on, like puriri, taraire and kohekohe, were disappearing. Some of the smaller birds found enough food and protection in the steep forest valleys that had been left uncleared. But most of the larger birds, like pigeons and kaka, which needed a greater area of forest, left their home on Tiritiri and migrated to other offshore islands or to the mainland, in search of more 'food' trees as well as the old trees with safe crevices to nest in.

With the forest birds gone or sheltered away in remaining pockets of steep forest, there was now very little birdsong, except for the distant calls of

sea birds. There was, however, the sound of the wind as it snarled in from the sea and swept across the flat, open grassland.

Above: A blue penguin and chicks nesting in a rocky cleft on the coast.

Opposite: One of the artificial nesting sites for blue penguin, alongside the coastal track.

Many large ships enter the busy Auckland harbour, and Tiritiri lies just out from the entrance to the harbour. Over a hundred years ago, as greater numbers of ships began calling in to Auckland, it became obvious that there were dangers in navigating through the rocky islands in the Gulf. There needed to be a prominent lighthouse, and the government decided that Tiritiri was the most obvious site for it.

And so, on this bare, pastured island, a lighthouse was built. At first, the lighthouse lamp was fuelled by whale oil, until 60 years later, when acetylene gas was used. Nearly a hundred years after that the light was electrified. It then flashed more brightly than any other lighthouse in the southern hemisphere, with a beam that could be seen up to 35 km away. The Tiritiri lighthouse was the sentinel that guarded the Auckland harbour for 120 years.

A 12-hectare piece of land surrounded the

Top: The lighthouse, which was originally painted red, and the first two lighthouse-keepers' cottages. (Auckland Museum)

Above: The signal station being operated to identify ships entering the harbour. (Auckland Museum)

Left: A New Zealand native pigeon, one of the larger forest birds most affected by the clearance of the land.

THE LIGHTHOUSE

In 1864, a 20.5 m-high lighthouse was built on Tiritiri from prefabricated iron plates brought out from England. A team of 12 bullocks dragged the heavy plates up from the beach to the highest point of the island. These iron plates were fixed together with heavy bolts, and 20 mm-thick glass enclosed the light.

Cottages were built for two lighthouse keepers, who also grazed sheep and cattle in a 12-ha reserve. The lighthouse, painted red, was unveiled on 1 January 1865.

The first light was a wick lamp fuelled by whale oil, and this remained until an acetylene-burning fixed light was installed in 1925.

In 1947 the lighthouse was repainted white, and in 1955 the light was electrified, powered by a diesel generator. In 1956 an 11 million candle-power xenon lamp was donated by Sir Ernest Davis. It had eight beams, which flashed every 15 seconds, making it the most powerful light in the southern hemisphere. In 1967 an underwater main-power cable was laid, linking Tiritiri to the national power grid.

In April 1984, the Tiritiri light was automated when the xenon lamp was replaced by a smaller, less powerful quartz iodine lamp. The power cable was broken in 1986 and now the lighthouse is fully automated using solar power, producing a 300,000 candle-power beam.

lighthouse-keepers' houses. On this land each keeper was allowed to graze 50 sheep, two cows, one ram, one bull, 12 hens and six ducks. And each year, the keepers were required to send in a stock return to the Lighthouse Service with these exact details!

When ships and boats began using their own radar systems to guide them in and out of the harbour, the very bright light from the lighthouse was no longer needed, and a smaller quartz iodine lamp was installed. Later, when the light became automatic, there was no longer a need for a lighthouse keeper.

Opposite: The lighthouse as it is seen today. In 1947 it was painted white.

The government owned Tiritiri but had leased it to farmers for a hundred years. When the lease expired they decided that there would be no more farming on the island and no more farm animals.

Conservationists said, 'Tiritiri should be left alone to grow wild once more, but someone needs to take care of the island. Perhaps Ray, the lighthouse keeper, could become the island keeper.'

And so Ray was appointed the Department of Conservation ranger and would continue to live on the island and be responsible for the welfare of the developing forest. But first he spent several years studying island management with the Department of Lands and Survey.

Scientists and rangers were excited about the possibilities for the island. 'If trees are allowed to grow up through the grass, Tiritiri could become a home for forest birds again.' They also planned that once the forest grew and the birds returned, visitors would be able to come to the island to see and hear them.

Karaka berries were some of the first berries to be collected from the old forest.

'This island could become an important sanctuary for endangered birds.' They knew that on the mainland many forest birds were in danger because early settlers had cleared so much native forest and introduced animals which hunted birds. In many places there was no control over the possums, stoats, cats and rats. Many thousands of possums fed in the mainland forests, eating tree fruits, berries, flowers and juicy shoots. Not only were these foods needed by the birds, but many trees also died.

'Here on Tiritiri,' they said, 'we can keep control over any predators.'

The island's forest was growing very slowly on its own, and the scientists could see that it would take a long time for it to become a real forest. Because the grassy land had been used for grazing for so long, the soil had become compacted and it was difficult for seeds to germinate in the hard soil. 'We need to help the trees along,' they said. 'The birds need lots of native trees close together, and we must get them growing as soon as possible.'

Now more plans were made — plans to *plant* a

new forest. The scientists devised a management plan; they knew what sort of trees were needed. 'It's very important that we plant the same types of trees that once grew all over the island. They will grow best here and be best for the birds. We'll gather berries from the trees in the old forest.'

'The first seedlings we'll plant will be pohutukawa,' the scientists decided. 'These grow quickly and will shade out the thick grass and stop it growing. Pohutukawa will also protect the slower-growing tree seedlings from the sun and wind.'

Ripe berries were gathered from trees and off the forest floor. Ray, who was now the island keeper, set up a nursery where he could plant the seeds from these berries. When the seedlings were big enough, they would be planted out and would eventually grow into tall, strong trees, spreading across the island and joining up with the old forest.

Within a year many seedlings had grown up in the nursery, but there were far too many for Ray to plant out on his own — he was going to need help if the new forest was to be a success.

NURSERY & REPLANTING

The nursery on Tiritiri was set up in 1983 and consisted of buildings and shadehouses located within the lighthouse complex. A landscape architect stayed on the island for over a year, helping with plans to set up the planting project.

Seeds gathered from remnants of the old forest were germinated in root trainers and stored in the shadehouse. After a year they were ready to be planted out.

With the help of many volunteers, the replanting programme began in 1984, and since then over 250,000 trees and shrubs have been planted. Each year, the nursery continues to produce approximately 20,000 shrub and tree seedlings

There were many people on the mainland who wanted to help restore the lost forest on Tiritiri. So during the autumn and winter, volunteer groups of school children and conservationists came by boat to help with the planting.

Ray explained how to plant the seedlings: 'First

Above: The plant nursery viewed from the lighthouse.

Opposite above: View across the new forest with flax in the foreground.

Opposite below: Ray Walter, the island keeper, attending to seedlings in the shadehouse of the nursery (left), and showing how a new tree should be planted (right).

you dig a small hole with a spade, then put the seedling in. It's important to tuck tufts of soft grass around the roots of each plant to protect them from the wind. Don't leave any bare earth.'

As they helped with the planting, these volunteers also became keepers of the new forest. Every little seedling was important because it would eventually provide food and shelter for many native birds.

After the planting of pohutukawa seedlings, one of the first shrubs to be planted was coprosma, which produces fruit over a long season. One coprosma branch produces a multitude of berries, and because the berries ripen at different times they provide a supply of fruit from summer through to winter.

The other early plantings were mahoe, kohekohe, puriri, karaka and cabbage tree seedlings. Puriri trees are valuable as they produce nectar-filled flowers and berries throughout the year. Within three years taraire, five finger and pigeonwood seedlings were also being planted.

The plans for the island were going well. Red-crowned parakeets were the first birds to be liberated into Tiritiri forest. Then a few years later bright, singing saddlebacks, which no longer lived on the mainland, were brought in from Cuvier Island off the coast of the Coromandel Peninsula.

When the new trees were still young, and bushes and long grass still grew over much of the island, two rare takahe were taken there. Although the birds did not need forest trees to feed from, they did need a sanctuary. The takahe were brought to Tiritiri from Maud Island in the Marlborough Sounds. These birds, named Mr Blue and Stormy, were bigger than roosters, and their deep blue and green feathers gleamed as brightly as the sea that splashed round the shores of the island.

Being friendly birds and used to humans, they were happy strutting about and feeding on sweet, juicy grass stems, fern rhizomes and fallen berries.

Right: A red-crowned parakeet feeding its mate by regurgitation. This pair are nesting in a cavity of a pohutukawa tree.

Top: *An immature saddleback, showing the undeveloped wattle.*

Above: *An adult takahe.*

THE TAKAHE

Takahe once inhabited areas of the North and South Islands, although 200 years ago the birds were only found in the Fiordland mountain region. Having evolved as a flightless bird, and also being large and plump, the takahe was easy prey for the first human hunters in New Zealand.

By the end of the nineteenth century takahe were thought to be extinct. However, in 1948, while tramping in the Murchison Mountains, west of Lake Te Anau, Dr W.R.B. Orbell noticed that snow tussock plants had been freshly chewed, and he also found takahe droppings among the plants.

After several expeditions to search for it, the takahe was rediscovered, having not been seen for 50 years. The population at this time was estimated to be about 200 birds. However, in the 1970s numbers declined.

In summer takahe feed among tussock plants, and in winter when snow covers much of the tussock, they move into the beech forest to feed mainly on fern rhizomes. But because introduced deer also feed on this vegetation, food for the birds in beech forests is scarce.

As the birds were not breeding successfully, takahe were classified as an endangered species — they needed to be moved to sanctuaries. Some were moved to two centres on the mainland and some to Maud Island. Tiritiri's first two takahe, Mr Blue and Stormy, were transferred from Maud Island in 1991.

Mr Blue, so familiar to visitors to Tiritiri, died in 1996, aged nearly 12.

The takahe pulled each grass stem out with their strong beaks then held the stem in one foot while they chewed at it.

One day Ray noticed them building a nest in a clump of grass. They were both male birds, but male takahe share in the nesting procedure. Ray placed a dummy egg in the nest and both birds dutifully took turns sitting on it. So it was decided to bring in a real egg from Maud Island and put it in the nest.

Mr Blue and Stormy were careful parents. They shared in incubating this egg until one day out hatched a little sooty-coloured chick, which was

Above: A sooty-coated takahe chick.

Opposite: A takahe feeding its chick. Chicks are fed frequently with small items of food.

named Matangi. Later, another adult takahe, a female named JJ, was introduced to the island. Tiritiri was now seen as a safe place for takahe, so two years later six more were moved there. From these first birds, the takahe population has continued to increase. Today, there are over 20 takahe on Tiritiri.

Mr Blue became an important identity on Tiritiri. Visitors became used to the sight of him wandering around the nursery, curious and fearless of humans. As a 'father figure' in the successful breeding programme and with his trust of visitors, he epitomised the achievement of Tiritiri as an open sanctuary.

This seemed like a good beginning. All the farm animals, cats and dogs had gone and the young trees were beginning to grow. But no one had realised just how much damage could be caused by the kiore, which still lived on the island. It was soon obvious what a problem they were in a forest; they nibbled at young shoots and seedlings, and ate insects needed by birds and lizards. They also climbed trees, creeping into birds' nests, where they cracked

the eggshells and sucked out the insides.

Kiore would have to be eradicated if Tiritiri was to be a really safe sanctuary. More plans had to be made, 'We will have to drop poison bait to kill them. But we must also protect the birds from any danger.'

And after just one helicopter drop of bait on Tiritiri, all the kiore were killed.

Above: An adult takahe bathing.

Below: Kiore, the Polynesian rat, which has now been eliminated from the island.

Opposite: A fantail feeding its newly fledged chicks. Until their wings are fully developed, the chicks move by fluttering from branch to branch.

The young trees grew faster once the kiore had been destroyed, spreading out strong branches of bright, new leaves. As the trees grew taller, fantails, silver-eyes, grey warblers and bellbirds were attracted out from the old forest. In the new forest they found extra food and many more branches for roosting and shelter.

By now karaka and kohekohe seedling trees were growing well. Birds were also helping to spread seeds naturally through the new forest. Many varieties of

trees were planted once they were ready to leave the nursery.

White-heads and robins were transferred to the island. Native pigeons flew across from the mainland as more forest food became available. Harrier hawks were sometimes seen hovering over the island, and moreporks called out at night. The island came alive again.

Spotless crakes hid during the day in the rushes of a swampy valley, coming out at dawn and dusk to feed on insects and worms. But pukeko preferred more open grassland, searching out shoots and grubs, and often sharing feeding grounds with the takahe. Kaka began to visit Tiritiri from Little Barrier Island, attracted by the abundance of pohutukawa flowers.

As the birds settled into the forest, some pecked the ripest berries, some sipped sweet nectar from the bell-like puriri and kowhai flowers, the cornet-shaped flax flowers and the fiery smothering of pohutukawa blooms. Others found insects on trees and under fallen leaf litter. Some birds fed on a

Top: Male bellbird drinking from the stream in 'Number 1 Bush'.

Above: A white-head. These birds were transferred from Little Barrier Island.

Opposite: Silver-eye on its nest. They are commonly seen on Tiritiri.

little of everything. The island had become a real home for them, and there was now something to sing about. They called to each other in soft chatterings, chortles and whistles. They sang out in their own new territories, chorusing with a special crescendo of song at nesting time in spring and summer. As the birds flew from tree to tree, feeding on nectar and berries, they also re-seeded and pollinated the forest. So the birds, too, became keepers of their island.

Only when trees are older do they form deep holes and crevices in their trunks and branches which birds can use for nesting sites. So, while the

Above: North Island robin. These birds are often seen in trees and on the ground close to the visitors' walkway.

Right: North Island robin pulling a worm from the leaf litter.

Opposite: Kaka visit the island to feed. Nest boxes have been built to encourage the birds to nest there.

trees were still young, nest boxes were provided for the birds, and with each new season their numbers increased.

Young chicks knew this forest as the *only* forest. They had never lived anywhere else, and all they needed was here. It was now noticeable that since the kiore had been destroyed, many more chicks were surviving.

Tiritiri had now become accepted as a successful island sanctuary, so rangers and scientists considered other birds that needed protection. Little spotted kiwi are found only on Kapiti Island and a few other small islands off the New Zealand mainland. Because they cannot protect themselves from predators like stoats and wild cats, the only way to save the species has been to transfer them to safe islands, so rangers brought a few pairs to the safe sanctuary of Tiritiri.

Left above: A male stitchbird feeding on coprosma berries.

Left below: A nectar feeding table for stitchbirds. The netting excludes larger birds.

Left: A bellbird singing.

Below left: Arrival by helicopter of the little spotted kiwi.
(Shaun Dunning)

Below right: Little spotted kiwi feeding among leaf litter.

Above: Brown teal on the pond habitat they favour.

Opposite: A pair of brown teal resting at the small pond above the wharf.

Below: Kingfisher carrying a spider to its nest hole in the clay bank near the wharf.

THE BROWN TEAL

Brown teal live quite happily on Great Barrier Island, although they are usually found on rivers in the north. But because farmers clear vegetation from the banks of these waterways, the small native ducks lose their important source of food and shelter. Stoats and cats also catch them, and rats take their eggs.

More plans were made. 'We could create ponds by damming up small gullies. These would be safe places for the rare brown teal.' So diggers were brought over from the mainland by barge to scoop out hollows to form ponds. Eight ponds have now been created. Brown teal have settled here happily, free from introduced predators and with a good supply of water insects to feed on as well as the lush grasses that drape the edges of the ponds and trail into the water. They nest in the clumps of grass and vegetation which surround the ponds and roost in this during the day, so they may sometimes be difficult to see.'

Above: A copper skink sunning itself. Skinks also feed on insects and grubs.

Opposite above: A fantail at its nest. The adult bird shows the 'fanned tail'.

Opposite below: A stick insect, sometimes eaten by tui, saddlebacks and kingfishers.

Also living in these ponds are eels and banded kokopu. Kingfishers dive for these small native fish, although they feed as readily on insects and skinks. Kingfishers have tunnelled out nesting holes in a clay bank near the wharf at Tiritiri.

As the trees grew, they spread out to form a thick,

shady forest. The forest became a home not only for birds, insects and spiders, but also for skinks, which live under old leaves, roots and rocks. Now that all the kiore have gone, skinks are sometimes seen sunning themselves on the boardwalk.

Visitors are able to watch and listen to the birds as they feed, flicker through branches and splash in a trickling stream. Small insect-eating birds may dart close to the pathway as visitors sometimes disturb the leaf litter where many insects live. As fantails flit through the branches, they feed on flying insects, which they catch in the air, and their 'fanned tail' may act as a sweeper, whisking insects from leaves and bark. Fantails also follow saddlebacks and white-heads as they fossick for insects in the foliage and bark of trees, with the fantails snatching the flying insects that are disturbed.

Welcome swallows flew across to Tiritiri on their own and may be seen skimming over the ponds after flying insects, or dipping and diving along the shoreline as they feed on kelp flies.

Above: The bush boardwalk where it crosses the main stream.

Opposite: Tui sipping nectar from a kowhai.

At first, visitors walked along tracks through the old forest, called 'Number 1 Bush', but the rangers and scientists soon realised that footsteps could damage tree roots, so a wooden walkway was built through the forest with help from volunteers.

Soon the number of forest birds whose ancestors had once lived on Tiritiri increased, along with others that had been given sanctuary on the island. Tui and bellbirds were now frequently seen, and a third 'honeyeater', the stitchbird, which lives in safety on Little Barrier Island, was also brought to Tiritiri. To help the stitchbird make a ready home on the island, flasks of sugar water were left out among the trees.

And as the 'food trees' grew and Tiritiri forest became an established, sheltered place again,

THE WATTLEBIRDS

The three wattlebirds of New Zealand, of ancient lineage, are the huia, which is now extinct, the saddleback and the kokako. They are called 'wattlebirds' because of the colourful, fleshy wattles at the gape of their beaks.

The saddleback once inhabited forests throughout mainland New Zealand, but predation by rats, cats and stoats, and possibly exotic diseases, has meant they now survive only on offshore island sanctuaries. The bird often searches among leaf litter and under flaking bark for insects, grubs and spiders, as well as feeding on fruit.

The kokako lives in some lowland forests of the North Island. It is a weak flier, bounding through the forest as it feeds on foliage, flowers and fruit, and small insects. It appears that the South Island kokako may be extinct.

Because of predation, particularly by the possum, a number of kokako have been transferred to sanctuaries on Little Barrier, Kapiti Island and others, as well as a few more recently to Tiritiri Island.

Kokako are renowned for their hauntingly beautiful song.

THE HONEYEATERS

In New Zealand there are three birds that are classed as honeyeaters (nectar feeders): the tui, bellbird and stitchbird. These birds have a special long, brush-tipped tongue to help them sip up nectar from inside flowers. The main trees and shrubs that bear these nectar-laden flowers are: kowhai, pohutukawa, puriri, rata, flax and kohekohe. They also eat fruit and insects, particularly when feeding chicks.

Birds like silver-eye, kaka and parakeet also occasionally take nectar. Although they do not have a long, brush tongue, they are able to take nectar from more open flowers.

scientists decided that the island could also be a sanctuary for the very endangered kokako. The kokako is an ancient wattlebird, related to the saddleback and the extinct huia. Kokako are weak fliers, so as they feed they spring from branch to branch, rather like squirrels.

On the mainland, predators like possums, stoats and feral cats often attack the kokako and climb into their nests, taking eggs and killing chicks. Possums also feed on the flowers and fruit — food that is needed by the kokako.

So if these birds are to survive they need protection from predators. In 1997, the first three kokako were released on Tiritiri Island, followed by another five young birds in 1998. As the kokako call to each other, their song is like the music of flutes, echoing through the trees.

The forest, once lost on Tiritiri but restored by many volunteers, has become the new forest. The

Above left: A tui singing in a kowhai tree.

Opposite: The North Island kokako.

sounds of birdsong, which are not often heard on the mainland and were once lost on Tiritiri, are heard here again. Tiritiri Matangi has become 'The Singing Island'.

From the island you can look below to the deep jade-blue sea and out across the Pacific Ocean. In the distance the city of Auckland, with a million people, can be seen clearly. But from the forested island, singing with birds, it seems far, far away.

Right: A view from the island.

Appendix 1

Important food trees and shrubs

All the trees that have been planted on Tiritiri provide food for birds. The fast-growing pohutukawa were the first seedling trees to be planted so they could form a protective canopy over the other slower-growing trees.

The nectar-filled flowers usually bloom from spring through summer, and during autumn and into winter the berries ripen. Insect food is more readily available from spring through until autumn. In the cooler winter months there are only a few grubs or caterpillars and many insects hibernate so it is more difficult for birds to search them out.

Many forest birds feed on a wide variety of these

berries, leaves, shoots, flowers and insects, depending on their seasonal availability.

Berries

Trees and shrubs which bear fruit are considered particularly valuable, because they provide a rich food source for so many forest birds. The earliest berry-producing seedlings to be planted were coprosma, mahoe, kohekohe, puriri and cabbage trees. Others planted later were taraire, karaka, and five finger.

Of these, the two especially important trees are the coprosma, which bears fruit that ripens through summer and on into winter, and the puriri, which produces berries as well as nectar flowers throughout the year. The larger puriri, karaka and taraire berries are a favourite food of the native pigeon.

Kokako also eat these large berries as well as supplejack berries from vines that entangle some of the mature trees in the old forest. Nikau palms are now growing well and these produce huge bouquet sprays of shiny red fruit, much loved by pigeons.

Above: Kaka chewing on a coprosma stem.

Opposite above: Coprosma have a long fruiting season.
Opposite below: Mahoe berries.

Nectar

Important trees and shrubs bearing nectar flowers have been planted on Tiritiri. Perhaps the most prominent of these is the pohutukawa, with puriri, kowhai, kohekohe, rewarewa and flax also providing a plentiful variety of food for the nectar feeders.

Large, mature kohekohe trees also exist in the old forest. These trees are unusual in that they produce tiny, white nectar-filled flowers followed by bunches of large, green berries like grapes, which grow directly from the trunk. Kohekohe flowers produce a very rich, sugary nectar, particularly favoured by the bellbird.

The claret-coloured rewarewa flower, formed as a cluster of stamens and curled knots, is also known as New Zealand honeysuckle. Like the pohutukawa, the stamens of the rewarewa flower spread outward from tiny cups of nectar. This makes it easier for birds with shorter tongues to feed from them.

Flowers & Shoots

The flowers of some trees and shrubs, particularly kowhai, are a favourite food and offer variety for

Above: Rewarewa flower, which produces nectar.

birds like pigeons and kaka. Leaves are also eaten by some birds, with the kokako feeding on a wide selection of flowers, buds and shoots.

The red-crowned parakeet, as well as feeding on fruits and leaves, also chews at the aerial roots of the pohutukawa. Seeds are important in the parakeet's diet and on the island the birds especially enjoy the abundance of flax seeds.

Insects

Trees play a vital role in hosting the insects and spiders that live under loose bark and on foliage.

Opposite above: Puriri flowers and fruit are both produced throughout the year.

Opposite below: Supplejack fruit — much favoured by the kokako.

Many nectar- and fruit-feeding birds eat insects, especially when feeding chicks, as this supplies the growing chicks with the extra protein they need.

Others like the saddleback feed widely on a diet of fruit and nectar as well as insects. Saddlebacks like to feed on insects that live in the crown of cabbage trees, and the kaka uses its strong beak to rip off loose bark in search of grubs and beetles.

Some birds like fantails, robins and grey warblers feed only on insects. The white-head feeds mainly on insects but may also take fruit and seeds.

As forest trees drop their leaves, valuable 'leaf litter' is formed on the forest floor. Insects, spiders, worms, grubs and skinks make a home in this leaf litter, and in turn insectivorous birds find food there. At night, the little spotted kiwi probes with its long bill into the soft earth and leaf litter for insects and worms, feeding as well on ripe, fallen berries.

Pollination

Birds play a vital part in the reproduction of the forest. After digesting berries, they disperse the seeds in their droppings, and as birds sip up nectar, pollen from the flowers coats their upper beak and is transferrred as they feed from flower to flower, resulting in pollination.

During the day the variations of colour from red and yellow, pink and orange through to deep ink-purple of both the flowers and berries, are most obvious within the forest trees, attracting birds to feed. But birds will search through the forest for other less conspicuous ripened berries, feeding just as readily on the palest coloured fruit.

Bees also sip nectar, carrying pollen with them and assisting with pollination, and at night, moths are lured to the sweet-scented, light-coloured flowers. In this way all flowers are fertilised.

Thirty-eight different species of seedlings have been raised in the nursery and planted to create the new forest.

The planting of food trees continues, complemented with natural reseeding and the maturing growth of this new forest.

Above: A coastal pohutukawa tree.

Opposite above: The flax flower produces valuable nectar for the tui.

Opposite below: The highly scented cabbage tree flower.

Appendix 2

Birds of Tiritiri Island

Seventy-six species of birds have been seen on or close to Tiritiri.

- Seven of these are endangered species in New Zealand (transferred to the island)
- Nineteen birds, endemic or indigenous to New Zealand, may be seen on or near Tiritiri, but are not known to breed on the island.
- Twenty-seven birds, endemic or indigenous to New Zealand, may be seen on or near Tiritiri and are known to breed on the island.
- Twenty-one birds that have been introduced into New Zealand have found their own way to the island. Not all are known to nest on the island.

Above: A saddleback feeding on a grub.

ENDANGERED BIRDS NOW ON TIRITIRI MATANGI

BROWN TEAL (Threatened)
- Over 1,000 exist on Great Barrier Island in the wild
- A few live on some Northland rivers
- Now on Tiritiri Matangi
- Threats: Clearing of habitat, predation by stoats, cats and black rats

RED-CROWNED PARAKEET (Threatened)
- Common on most offshore islands
- Uncommon in mainland forests
- Now on Tiritiri Matangi
- Threats: Competition for nest sites from other birds such as starlings. Predation by cats and stoats

SADDLEBACK (Threatened)
- The saddleback is now successful but only on offshore islands
- The last natural surviving population only existed on Hen Island, but since 1965 they have been transferred to nine predator-free islands
- Now on Tiritiri Matangi
- Predators: Stoats, cats and black rats

LITTLE SPOTTED KIWI (Endangered)
- Only common on Kapiti Island, where over 1,000 exist
- Also on predator-free islands like Red Mercury and Hen Islands
- Now on Tiritiri Matangi
- Predators: Cats, stoats and dogs

KOKAKO (Highly endangered)
- Population estimated to be less than 1,500 (not all areas surveyed yet)
- In the wild kokako are doing well in the predator-controlled forests of the King Country and Rotoehu
- Kokako also occur in forests in the Coromandel, Puketi, Pureora, Urewera, Hunua and Mamaku. Also on Little Barrier Island, Kapiti Island, Mt Bruce (on the mainland) sanctuaries
- Now on Tiritiri Matangi
- Predators: Possum, stoat and black rat

STITCHBIRD (Highly Endangered)
- Last natural surviving population existed only on Little Barrier Island
- Also on Kapiti and other predator-free offshore islands.
- Predators: Cats and black rats

TAKAHE (Highly Endangered)
- A total population of less than 200 birds
- Approximately 140 birds exist in the wild in the Fiordland Mountains area
- Some breeding at Burwood Sanctuary and a few at Mt Bruce on the mainland
- Some on Maud, Mana and Kapiti Islands, and over 20 on Tiritiri Matangi
- Threats: Deer competing for food, predation by stoats

TIRITIRI MATANGI: AN OPEN SANCTUARY

Every day ships, yachts and launches pass by Tiritiri Island as they enter or leave the busy Auckland harbour. Because the island is an open sanctuary, anyone may stop to visit. Tiritiri is close enough for day trips, with ferries sailing regularly throughout the year, from Princes Wharf in the city or from Gulf Harbour on the Whangaparaoa Peninsula.

Visitors learn about wild birds by seeing them as they flitter close by, feeding and singing. They see how it is possible to create a forest that provides food and shelter for birds. They also see that the island remains a home for birds that feed outside the forest on the seeds and leaves of tall grasses, and continues to be a roosting place for sea birds that come and go on the rocky shore.

Keeping means 'caring' and 'protecting.' Over 20,000 visitors a year call in to explore the island, so all who visit and care can become keepers. The birds here trust that they will always be safe on Tiritiri Island.

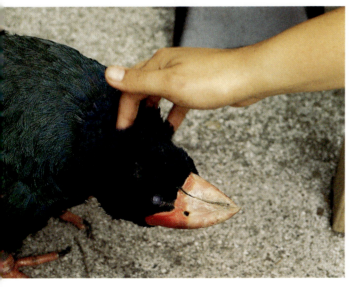

HOW TO GET THERE

M.V. TE AROHA operates specialist Bird Island tours, including a day on Tiritiri, from November until April. Contact Adventure Cruising Co.

FULLERS FERRIES operate throughout January, February and March on selected dates.

GULF HARBOUR FERRIES operate all year on Saturday, Sunday and Thursday. Ferries leave from Auckland and Gulf Harbour (Whangaparaoa).

SUPPORTERS OF TIRITIRI MATANGI

In 1988 an organisation of Tiritiri Supporters was formed. Members are involved in weekend events, meetings and contributions to management, with a regular news bulletin keeping supporters informed about the island's developments.

Membership is open to anyone interested in the support of Tiritiri Island. Contact: Ray and Barbara Walter, telephone 09 479 4490.

Top: A takahe wandering around visitors' bags.

Above: A takahe enjoying its neck being scratched.

Page 60: White-fronted terns in flight.

Opposite: Visitors arriving on the island by ferry.

Further Reading

The Reed Field Guide to New Zealand Birds, Geoff Moon, Reed, 1992

Field Guide to the Birds of New Zealand, Barrie Heather and Hugh Robertson, Viking, 1997

The Reed Field Guide to New Zealand Native Trees, J.T. Salmon, Reed, 1986

Which Native Tree?, Andrew Crowe, Viking, 1992

Which Native Forest Plant?, Andrew Crowe, Viking, 1994